YEAR OF THE OJIBWA

by Sharman Apt Russell
illustrated by Carlos Caban

MODERN CURRICULUM PRESS
Pearson Learning Group

It is the 1800s. A snow storm is blowing hard outside your wigwam. You are a small boy and your father asks you to step out of your family's cozy home to "shoot the snow." He puts a piece of birch bark on the end of a sharp arrow. Then he sets the birch bark on fire and fits the arrow to a bow.

"Go outside," he urges you. "Hit the snow right in the eye."

You step out of the wigwam as he watches. You shoot your arrow into the night, into the thickly falling snow.

Then you hurry back inside and go immediately to bed. Your mother promises that when you awake, the snowstorm will be gone. You fall asleep quickly, pleased and proud.

"Shooting the snow" is an Ojibwa (Oh-JIB-way) tradition. The Ojibwa are a large Native American tribe. They once farmed, fished, hunted, and gathered wild food around the Great Lakes. Today, many Ojibwa still live and work there.

Like most Native Americans, the Ojibwa treasure their traditions. They keep many of the customs that link them to their past. The Ojibwa speak an Algonquian (al-GONG-kwee-in) language. At one time, several hundred tribes spoke a language related to Algonquian.

Wigwam is the Algonquian word for "house." Traditionally, Ojibwa women built the winter wigwam. They set long poles into the ground and tied them at the top with strips of bark. Then they covered this frame of poles with mats made of cattails or other plants. The roof of the wigwam formed a dome, which they covered with more birch bark. Parents, children, and grandparents could all sleep and eat together in this snug home.

Winter nights were for working and storytelling. The men repaired snowshoes and animal traps. The women made cord, fish nets, and birch-bark dishes. The children played with dolls and toys. A fire burned low in the middle of this round, comfortable room.

The traditional Ojibwa had some customs similar to modern ones. When a child lost a tooth, the family would laugh and congratulate him or her. The Ojibwa, however, did not have a "tooth fairy." Instead, the child held the tooth in one hand and a piece of charcoal in the other hand. Then he or she threw the charcoal to the east and the tooth to the west. Next the child said loudly, "I want a new tooth as soon as possible!"

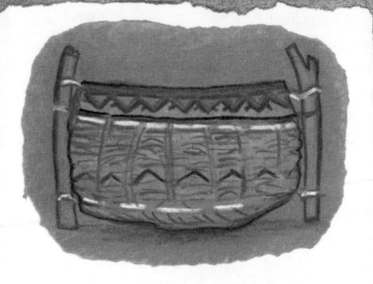

Historically, winter was time to prepare for one of the family's most important traditions—sugar mapling. The children helped make many birch-bark baskets. These would catch the maple sap. John Rogers, an Ojibwa boy who lived in the late nineteenth century, wrote that he and his sisters made over a thousand baskets every winter!

The Ojibwa say that they learned about maple sugar a long time ago from watching a black bear. The bear is thought to be a very wise animal. An ancestor of the Ojibwa saw a black bear scraping a tree and licking the sap. So the Ojibwa also went to the maple tree and tasted the sweet sap. The people knew the bear had given them a wonderful present.

In the early spring, a traditional Ojibwa family would go to their special stand of maple trees. They called this place a "sugar bush." Sometimes they walked a long way through the forest to get there. They carried their sugar mapling supplies in heavy packs.

The sugar bush of each Ojibwa family had an invisible boundary. No one else would use this family's special stand of trees. First the family made a hole in the trees and let the sap drip into baskets. Then they boiled the sap to make a rich heavy syrup. Next they poured the syrup into birch bark molds that were shaped in various forms. They cooled these "maple cakes" in the snow. They also stirred and beat some of the syrup to make maple sugar.

John Rogers wrote, "We worked all day like beavers!" He also remembers eating maple sugar, a favorite treat, all year round.

Today many Ojibwa families still go sugar mapling. Instead of birch-bark baskets, they usually use plastic buckets or other modern containers. They drill a hole in the bucket and put in tubes to allow the sap to drip into the containers.

Many modern Ojibwa still use maple syrup in traditional recipes. They may cook sweet potatoes and wild rice with syrup. They may pour maple syrup on wild rice pancakes. Some still mold maple cakes into the shapes of birds and leaves. They give these candies away as gifts to family and friends.

John Rogers' favorite season was spring. When maple sugaring was over, the family carried their packs back to the wigwam. Shoots of bright green grass covered the brown earth. Pale green rice grass grew along the lake. Purple violets filled the forest floor.

In a book about his childhood, John Rogers wrote, "The robin had already perched himself in trees wherever there was a ray of sunlight and in the pine and oak and birch that surrounded our wigwam. Here he sang his joyous song of welcome."

Spring was the best time to strip birch bark from the trees. The older children helped with this chore. Soon the wigwam was covered with a fresh, new roof. The Ojibwa also made lightweight canoes out of birch bark. They laid the bark on the ground and flattened it with stones. Then they pulled the bark and shaped it onto a frame of poles. They water-proofed the seams of the canoe with spruce or pine gum. It took about two weeks to make the canoe.

As the nights grew warmer, an Ojibwa family of times past would sit outside and marvel at the constellations in the sky. These groups of stars helped the Ojibwa tell the time of night and the seasons of the year. They studied the heavens carefully. Many constellations had names like "bear head" and "bear back." Sometimes the huge night sky seemed to go on forever, without a boundary.

In the summer, the Ojibwa children spent most of their time outdoors, just as children of all ages do today. They swam in the lake all day long. They also played hide and seek, marbles, and tag. They had races and games of sport.

Some children played at "calling the butterflies." Children were taught not to harm butterflies. Instead, they "called them in" to join their games. Children would hold their noses between a finger and thumb. Then they would run about crying "Butterfly, butterfly!" in a high voice.

In times past, a baby born in the summer was considered to be good luck. Sometimes relatives came to the wigwam to "kidnap" the baby. The parents threw water and flour at the pretend kidnappers. The men wrestled. Everyone laughed and joked.

Finally the "kidnappers" took the baby. They walked the baby around a fire four times. The people sang a song. They sang, "We have caught the little bird!" The parents of the baby gave gifts to the kidnappers to get their child back.

Later, the baby was put in a cradle board. The baby was bound firmly to the wooden board. Now the baby could be carried easily. The Ojibwa baby felt safe and protected.

At this time, the baby might also be given a nickname. A baby who scratched herself might be called Little Cat. A baby with a round face might be called Little Bear. These baby names sometimes lasted until that baby was an old man or woman!

When fall came, the Ojibwa women gathered wild rice. Two women sat in a canoe. One bent the rice plants over the canoe. The second hit the rice with a stick. Some rice fell into the canoe. Some rice fell into the lake to grow again for the next year.

Fall was also a good time to hunt and set animal traps. The Ojibwa needed animal meat and skins to get through the winter.

John Rogers remembers many good days hunting with his uncle. "Our canoes made ripples on the water," he wrote. "They made a beautiful sight. Our hearts were glad just to be there."

The Ojibwa mainly hunted deer, moose, fox, and wolf. They used bows and arrows. They made the bows from hickory and ash. Then they decorated the wooden bows with a red dye. They used traps and nets for otter, beaver, and mink.

When game was hard to find, a hunter might paint his face black. He would not eat before hunting or during hunting. His older children went with him, but he would also ask his younger children to paint their faces black. He would also ask the younger children not to eat while he was gone. The Ojibwa believed this would make the hunt more successful.

When winter came again, snow would fall. There would be heavy storms. When the "summer babies" grew older, they would be asked to go outside and shoot a burning arrow.

Today the Ojibwa people no longer live in wigwams. Most do not hunt with a bow and arrow. But they do remember how their ancestors lived. They remember their customs and traditions. And they smile when they think of the children who went outside to "shoot the snow."